I'm a Good Reader

Sue Van Heurck and Noella Mackenzie

Illustrated by Claire Phipps

Dominie Press, Inc.

Publisher: Raymond Yuen
Series Editor: Stanley L. Swartz
Consultant: Adria F. Klein
Editor: Bob Rowland
Designers: Lois Stanfield and Vincent Mao
Illustrator: Claire Phipps

First published 1995
New Edition © 2001 Dominie Press, Inc.

Published by:

🔾 **Dominie Press, Inc.**

1949 Kellogg Avenue
Carlsbad, California 92008 USA

www.dominie.com

ISBN 1-56270-379-X

Printed in Singapore by PH Productions Pte Ltd
1 2 3 4 5 6 PH 03 02 01

ITP

I put my book down
when Dad and Mom
call me for breakfast.

At breakfast, Dad helps me read
about the basketball game
in the newspaper.

On the way to school,
I like to read all the signs
on the freeway.

At school, my favorite story
is *The Three Little Pigs*.
My teacher reads it over and over.
Then we get to read it, too.

We like our teacher.
We have a lot of fun
reading books and writing stories.

My teacher helps me
when I need help,
but I do most of it by myself
because I'm a good reader.

After school, I read to my mom,
my dad, my sister, and the cat.
I can read to my grandma and
grandpa, too.

At night, I help Dad and Mom read the recipes so we can cook dinner. I help with the cooking, too.

When it's bedtime, Mom and Dad
take turns reading to me. Then
I get to read to myself.

After the light is out,
I hide under the covers
with my flashlight and read
some more. I'm a good reader,
and reading is fun.